Pebble Plus

T0069572

# President Donald Trump

by Nick Robison

CAPSTONE PRESS
a capstone imprint

Pebble Plus is published by Capstone Press,
1710 Roe Crest Drive, North Mankato, Minnesota 56003
www.mycapstone.com

Copyright © 2017 by Capstone Press, a Capstone imprint. All rights reserved. No part of this publication may be reproduced in whole or in part, or stored in a retrieval system, or transmitted in any form or by any means, electronic, mechanical, photocopying, recording, or otherwise, without written permission of the publisher.

**Library of Congress Cataloging-in-Publication Data**
Cataloging-in-publication information is on file with the Library of Congress.
ISBN 978-1-5157-7895-0 (hardcover)
ISBN 978-1-5157-7896-7 (paperback)
ISBN 978-1-5157-7897-4 (eBook PDF)

**Editorial Credits**
Jessica Nelson, designer; Scott Burger, media researcher

**Photo Credits**
AP Photo: Mike Groll, 7; Getty Images: New York Daily News Archive, 11, Stringer/Amanda Edwards, 15, Stringer/Kena Betancur, cover; Library of Congress: 29 (all); Newscom: AdMedia/CNP/Ron Sachs, 21, Reuters/Brendan McDermid, 17, Sipa USA/Anthony Behar, 27, ZUMA Press/Judie Burstein, 5; Shutterstock: Christopher Halloran, 19, Evan El-Amin, 1, jiawangkun, 13, Joseph Sohm, 23, Lev Radin, 25, SINITAR, 9

## Note to Parents and Teachers

*President Donald Trump* supports national history standards related to people and culture. The images support early readers in understanding the text. The repetition of words and phrases helps early readers learn new words. This book also introduces early readers to subject-specific vocabulary words, which are defined in the Glossary section. Early readers may need assistance to read some words and to use the Table of Contents, Glossary, Read More, Internet Sites, and Index sections of the book.

Printed in the United States of America.
022017 010275R

# Table of Contents

Born into Business . . . . . 4
The Business World . . . . . 10
Family Life. . . . . 16
Change to Politics . . . . . 18
Winning the Election . . . . . 24
President Trump . . . . . 26

Facts about Donald Trump . . . . . 28
Glossary . . . . . 30
Read More . . . . . 31
Internet Sites. . . . . 31
Index . . . . . 32

# Born into Business

Donald Trump was born in New York City on June 14, 1946. He was the fourth of five children. Donald's father, Frederick, ran a company that built apartment buildings. His mother, Mary, worked with various charities.

Donald (center) with his father, Frederick, and his mother, Mary

When he was 13, Donald's parents sent him to a military school in New York. The school helped Donald set and reach goals. He also enjoyed playing baseball, soccer, and other sports at the school.

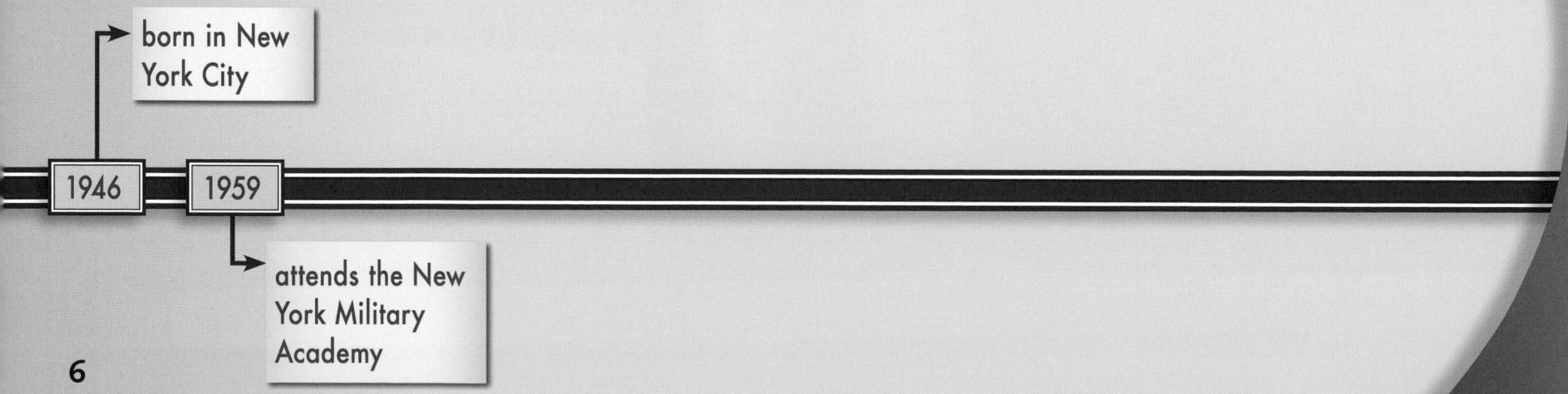

Donald in the 1964 yearbook from the New York Military Academy

After military school, Donald went to Fordham University in New York. Later he went to the Wharton School of the University of Pennsylvania. In 1968, Donald earned a college degree in economics.

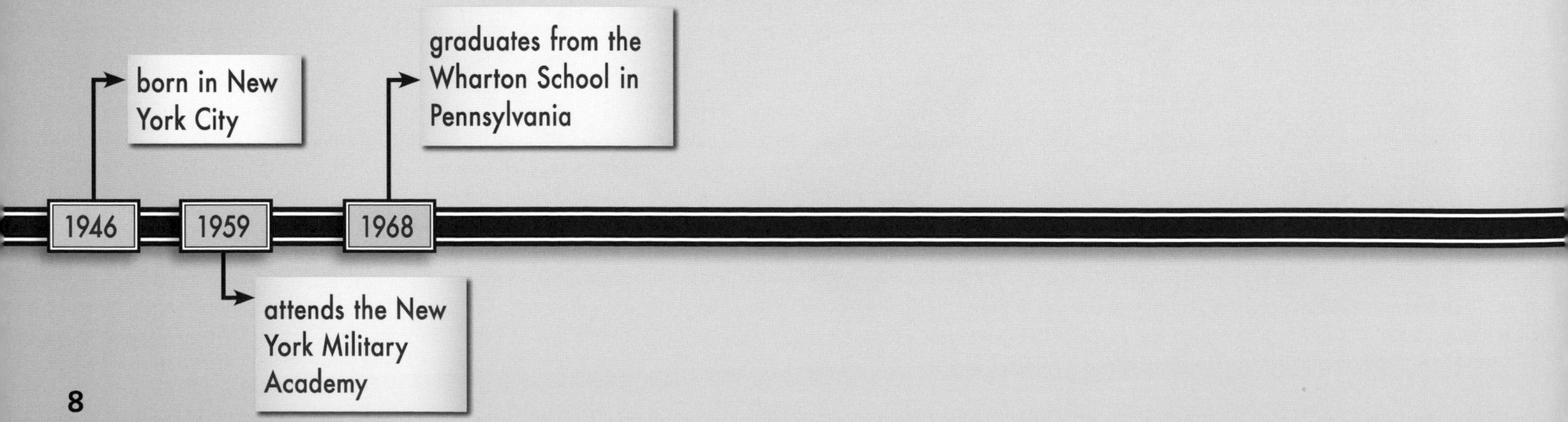

the Wharton School in Pennsylvania

# The Business World

In 1971, Donald took over his father's business. Soon he renamed it The Trump Organization. He bought, sold, and constructed many buildings. These included office buildings, hotels, and resorts. Donald earned a lot of money.

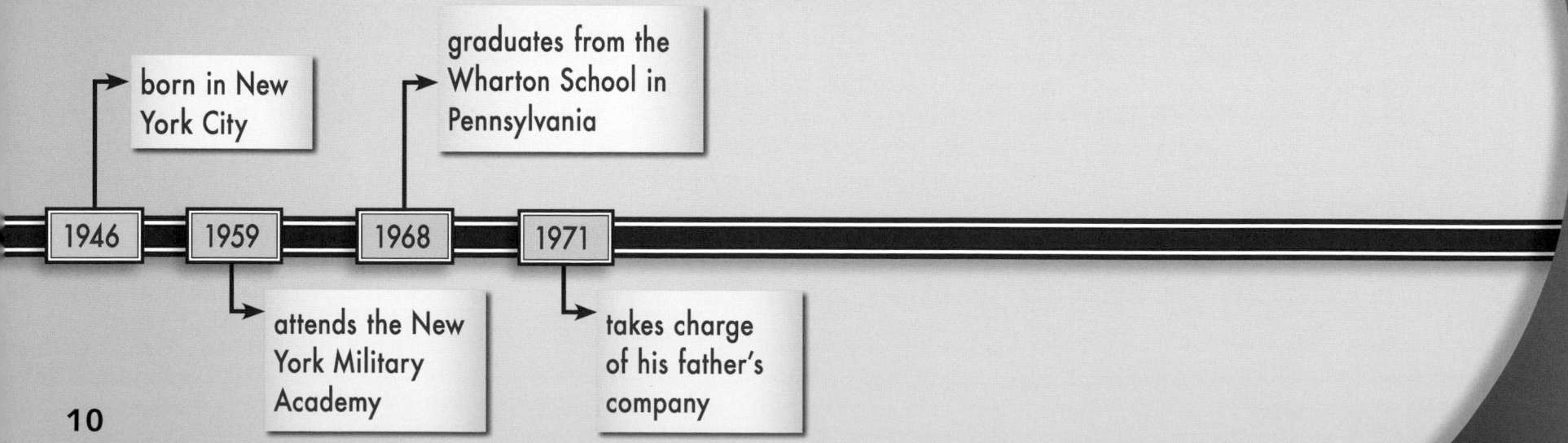

Donald announces plans for a convention center in New York in 1977.

Donald owns many fancy buildings in the United States and around the world. Many of the buildings have his last name on them. Donald has also written several books about business and his life.

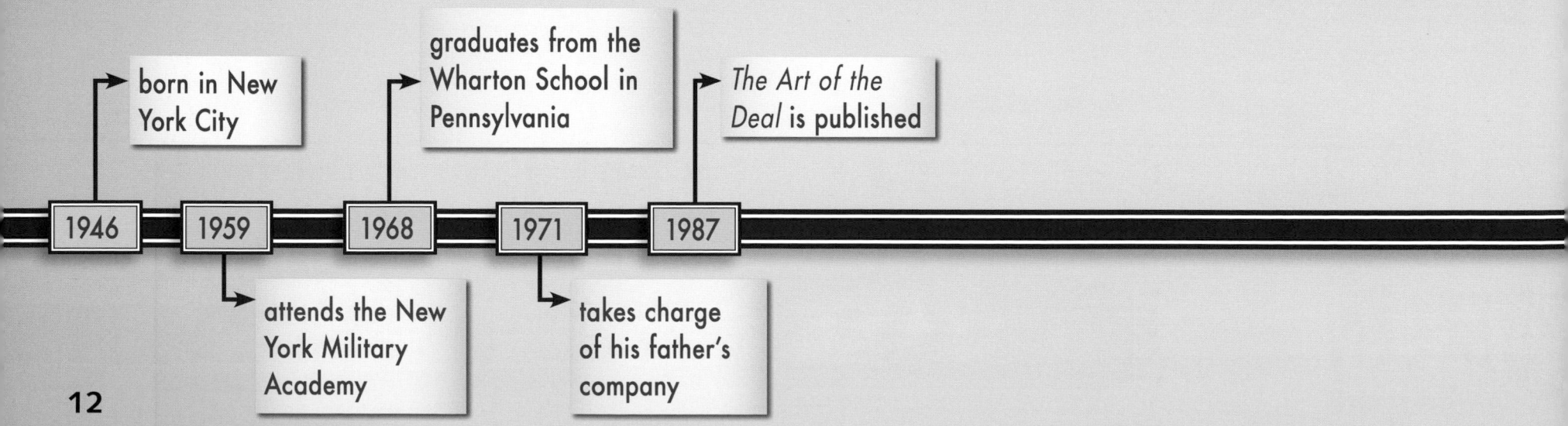

the main entrance to Trump Tower on Fifth Avenue in New York City

Donald also became a famous entertainer. He starred in his own reality TV show, *The Apprentice*. In the show, people tried to win a job working for Donald.

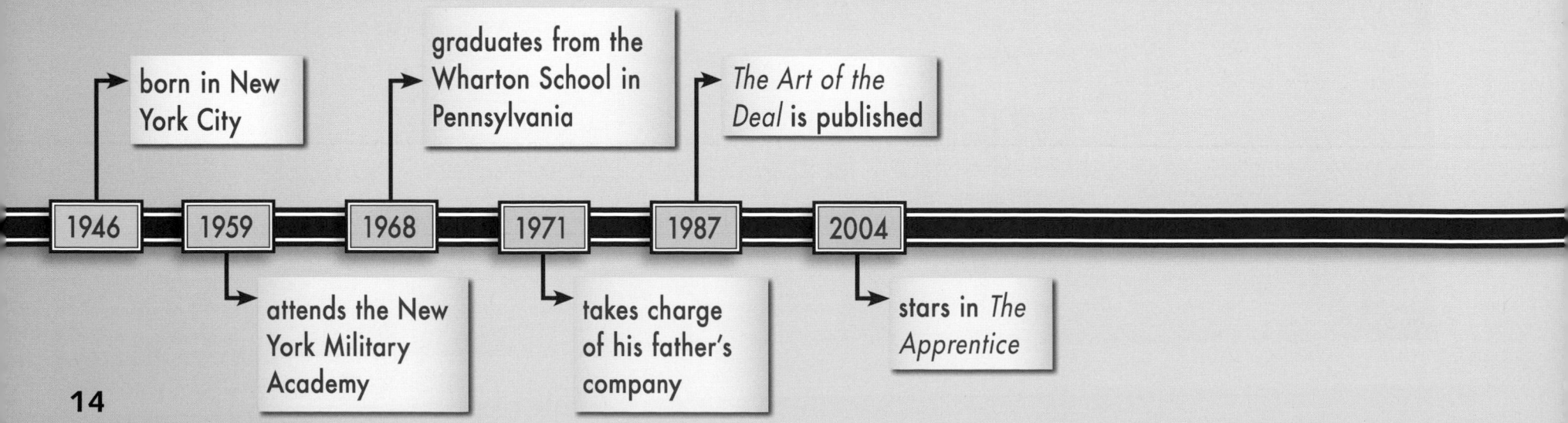

THE

# Family Life

Donald Trump has been married three times. He has five children. He married his current wife, Melania, in 2005. She used to be a model.

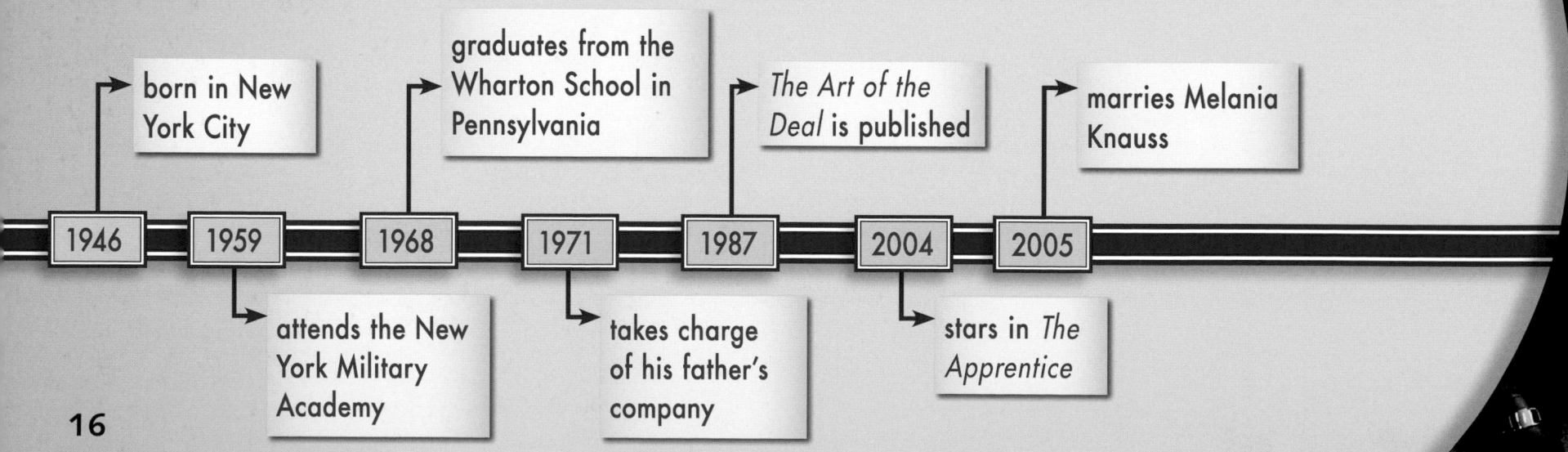

Donald Trump with his family

# Change to Politics

Over time, Donald became interested in politics. He thought about running for president several times. He also thought about running for governor of New York in 2006 and 2014.

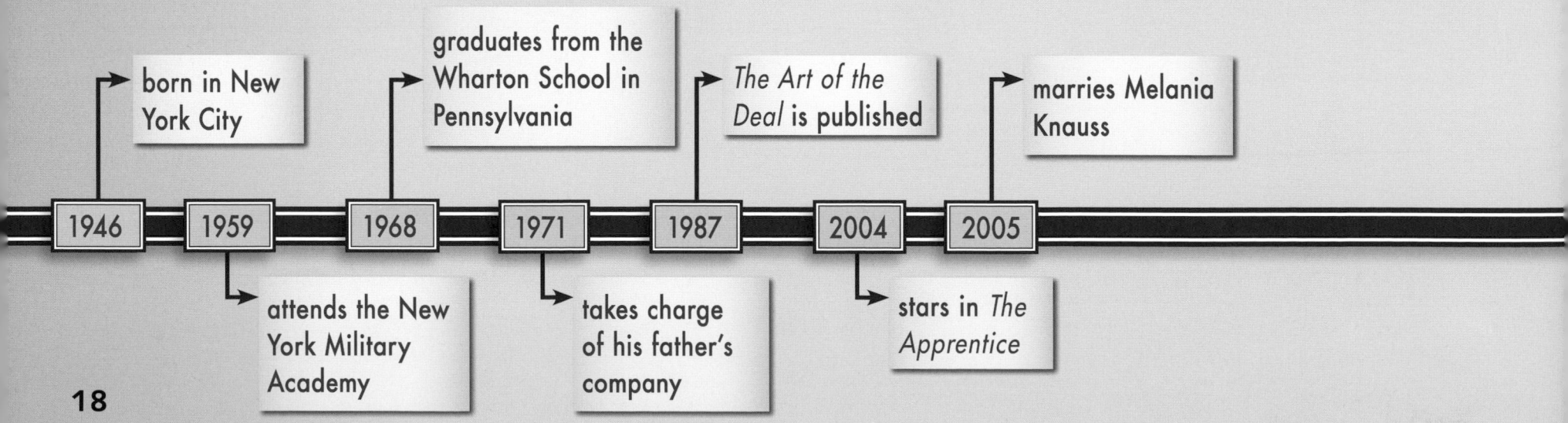

Conservative Political
Action Conference
CPAC
2014

Donald ran for president in 2016 as a Republican candidate. He had never held a political position before. He formed a team to help him win the campaign.

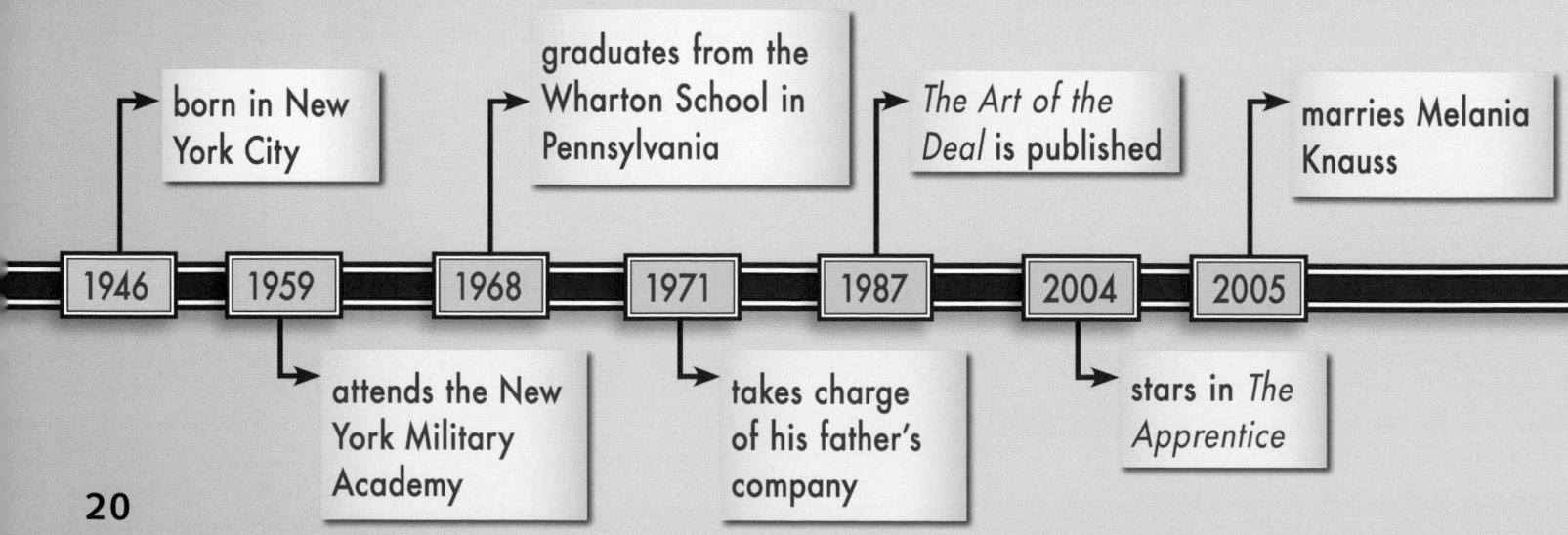

In July 2016, Donald Trump became the Republican presidential candidate.

Donald talked about making
more jobs available for workers.
He also covered health care,
keeping Americans safe,
and many other topics.
People were excited about the
changes he planned to make.

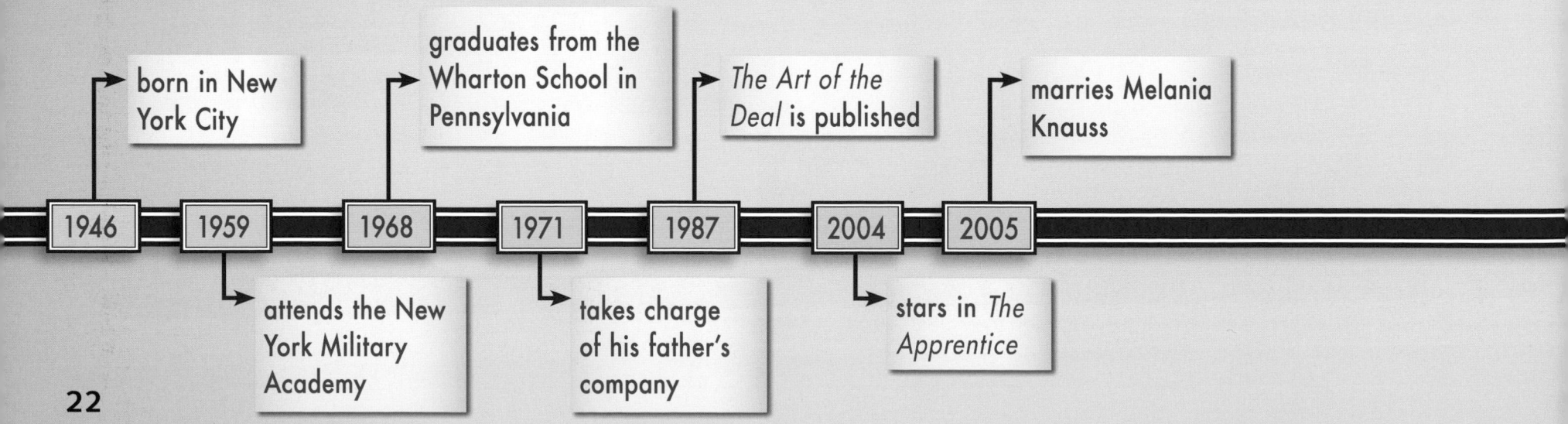

TRUMP
the silent majority
STANDS WITH
TRUMP
VETERANS
FOR
TRUMP
MAKE
AMERICA
GREAT AGAIN!

# Winning the Election

Americans voted on November 8, 2016. The next day, it was announced that Donald had won the election. He gave an acceptance speech in New York. The large crowd chanted, "USA! USA!"

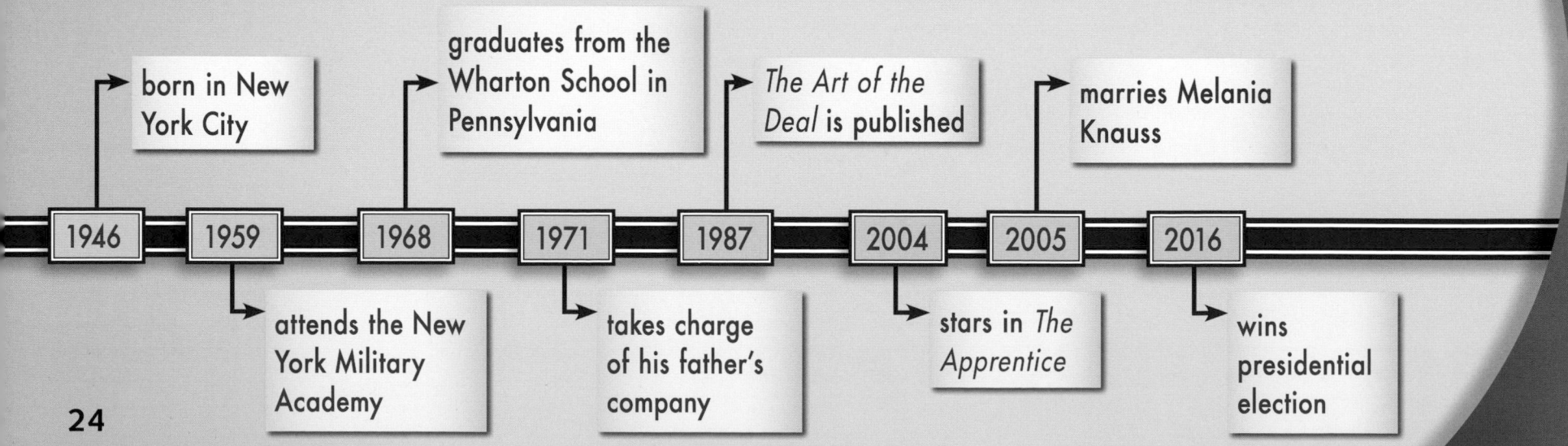

Donald gives a victory speech next to his wife, Melania, and son Barron.

# President Trump

Donald Trump became the 45th president on January 20, 2017. His slogan during the campaign was "Make America Great Again." Americans are excited to see what Donald can do to make that happen.

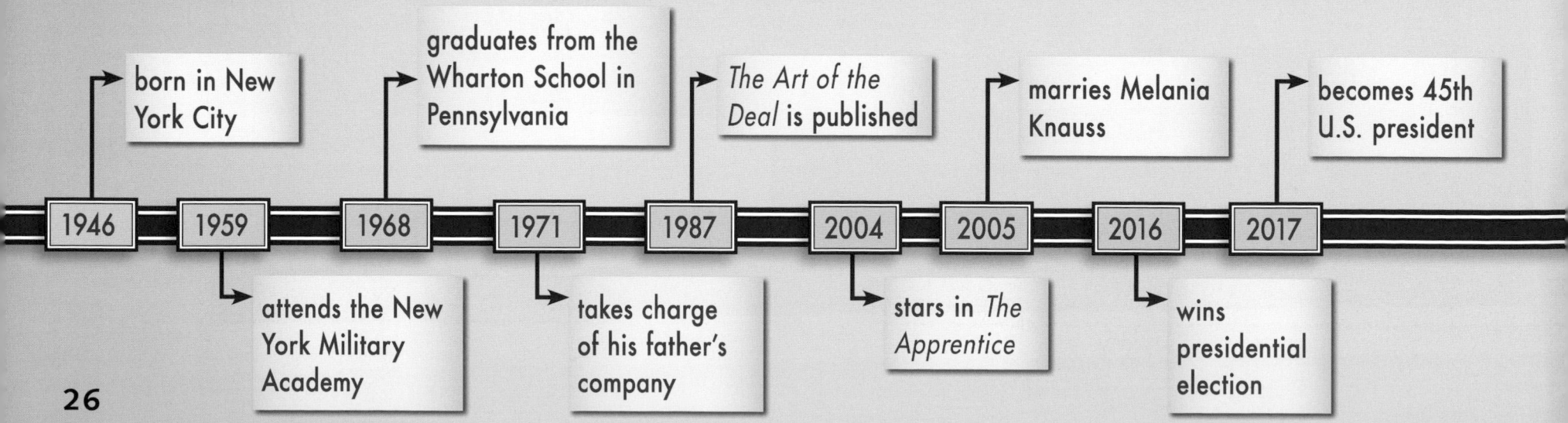

Donald Trump is sworn in as the 45th president of the United States.

# Facts about Donald Trump

**Born:**
June 14, 1946

**Parents:**
Frederick and Mary Trump

**Marriages:**
Ivana Zelníčková (1977–1992)
Marla Maples (1993–1999)
Melania Knauss (2005–present)

**Children:**
Donald Jr., born in 1977 (with Ivana Zelníčková)
Ivanka, born in 1981 (with Ivana Zelníčková)
Eric, born in 1984 (with Ivana Zelníčková)
Tiffany, born in 1993 (with Marla Maples)
Barron, born in 2006 (with Melania Knauss)

**Favorite movies:**
Donald has many favorite movies,
including *Citizen Kane* and *The Godfather*

**Favorite sport:**
Golf

**Nickname:**
The Donald

# Presidents of the United States

George Washington, 1789–1797
John Adams, 1797–1801
Thomas Jefferson, 1801–1809
James Madison, 1809–1817
James Monroe, 1817–1825
John Quincy Adams, 1825–1829
Andrew Jackson, 1829–1837
Martin Van Buren, 1837–1841
William Henry Harrison, 1841
John Tyler, 1841–1845
James K. Polk, 1845–1849
Zachary Taylor, 1849–1850
Millard Fillmore, 1850–1853
Franklin Pierce, 1853–1857
James Buchanan, 1857–1861
**Abraham Lincoln, 1861–1865**
Andrew Johnson, 1865–1869
Ulysses S. Grant, 1869–1877
Rutherford B. Hayes, 1877–1881
James A. Garfield, 1881
Chester Arthur, 1881–1885

Grover Cleveland, 1885–1889
Benjamin Harrison, 1889–1893
Grover Cleveland, 1893–1897
William McKinley, 1897–1901
Theodore Roosevelt, 1901–1909
William H. Taft, 1909–1913
Woodrow Wilson, 1913–1921
Warren G. Harding, 1921–1923
Calvin Coolidge, 1923–1929
Herbert Hoover, 1929–1933
Franklin D. Roosevelt, 1933–1945
Harry S. Truman, 1945–1953
Dwight D. Eisenhower, 1953–1961
**John F. Kennedy, 1961–1963**
Lyndon B. Johnson, 1963–1969
Richard M. Nixon, 1969–1974
Gerald R. Ford, 1974–1977
Jimmy Carter, 1977–1981
Ronald Reagan, 1981–1989
George H. W. Bush, 1989–1993
William J. Clinton, 1993–2001
George W. Bush, 2001–2009
Barack Obama, 2009–2017
Donald Trump, 2017–

# Glossary

**acceptance speech**—a speech a politician gives when he or she wins an election

**campaign**—actions and events done with a specific goal, such as an election

**candidate**—a person who runs for office, such as president

**charity**—a group that helps people in need

**construct**—to build

**election**—the act of choosing someone or deciding something by voting

**governor**—a person elected to be the head of a state's government

**reality TV**—a TV show without any scripts or professional actors

**vote**—to make a choice in an election

# Read More

**Lewison, Wendy Cheyette.** *P Is for President.* New York: Grosset & Dunlap, 2016.

**Stier, Catherine.** *If I Ran for President.* New York: AV2 by Weigl, 2013.

**Stine, Megan.** *Where Is the White House?* New York: Grosset & Dunlap, 2015.

# Internet Sites

FactHound offers a safe, fun way to find Internet sites related to this book. All of the sites on FactHound have been researched by our staff.

Here's all you do:

Visit *www.facthound.com*

Type in this code: 9781515778950

# Index

*Apprentice, The*, 14

birth, 4
books, 12
businesses, 4, 10, 12

campaigning, 20
children, 16

education, 6, 8
election, 24

father, 4
Fordham University, 8

governor, 18

health care, 22

jobs, 14, 22

marriages, 16
money, 10
mother, 4

New York City, 4, 8, 24

president, 18, 20, 26

safety, 22
slogan, 26
speeches, 24
sports, 6

Trump, Melania, 16
Trump Organization, The, 10

University of Pennsylvania, 8

voting, 24